Pebble Plus

Health and Your **Body**

Burps, Boogers, and Other Body Functions

by David Conrad

CAPSTONE PRESS
a capstone imprint

Pebble Plus is published by Capstone Press,
151 Good Counsel Drive, P.O. Box 669, Mankato, Minnesota 56002.
www.capstonepub.com

Library of Congress Cataloging-in-Publication Data
Conrad, David (David J.), 1967–
  Burps, boogers, and other body functions / by David Conrad.
     p. cm. — (Pebble plus. Health and your body)
  Includes bibliographical references and index.
  Summary: "Color photos and simple text describe body functions, such as gas, scabs, scars, and sweat"—Provided by
publisher.
  ISBN 978-1-4296-6808-8 (library binding)
  ISBN 978-1-4296-7125-5 (paperback)
  1. Human body—Juvenile literature. 2. Body fluids—Juvenile literature. 3. Hygiene—Juvenile literature. 4.
Health—Juvenile literature. I. Title. II. Series.
  QP37.C7882 2012
  612'.01522—dc22   2011005138

Editorial Credits
Gillia Olson, editor; Kyle Grenz, designer; Marcie Spence, media researcher; Laura Manthe, production specialist

Photo Credits
Alamy Images: David Knowles, 9; Capstone Studio: Karon Dubke, cover, 5, 7, 11, 15, 19, 21; iStockphoto Inc.:
nycshooter, 17; Shutterstock: Fedor Kondratenko, 13, Ilya Andriyanov, 1

Note to Parents and Teachers

The Health and Your Body series supports national science standards related to health and
physical education. This book describes and illustrates body functions. The images support early
readers in understanding the text. The repetition of words and phrases helps early readers learn
new words. This book also introduces early readers to subject-specific vocabulary words, which are
defined in the Glossary section. Early readers may need assistance to read some words and to use
the Table of Contents, Glossary, Read More, Internet Sites, and Index sections of the book.

Printed in the United States of America in North Mankato, Minnesota.
032011
006110CGF11

Table of Contents

Amazingly Gross!

The human body is amazing.
Sometimes we pass gas, burp,
and sweat. These body functions
might be funny. But there is a
reason for each of them.

Gas

Did you know you burp or
pass gas 10 to 15 times a day?
Food you eat breaks down
and makes gas. Gas is also
from swallowing air as you eat.

Ear Wax

Ear wax traps dust and germs

so they don't hurt your ear.

Let ear wax come out on its own.

Cleaning the ear canal can hurt

the ear or cause a wax plug.

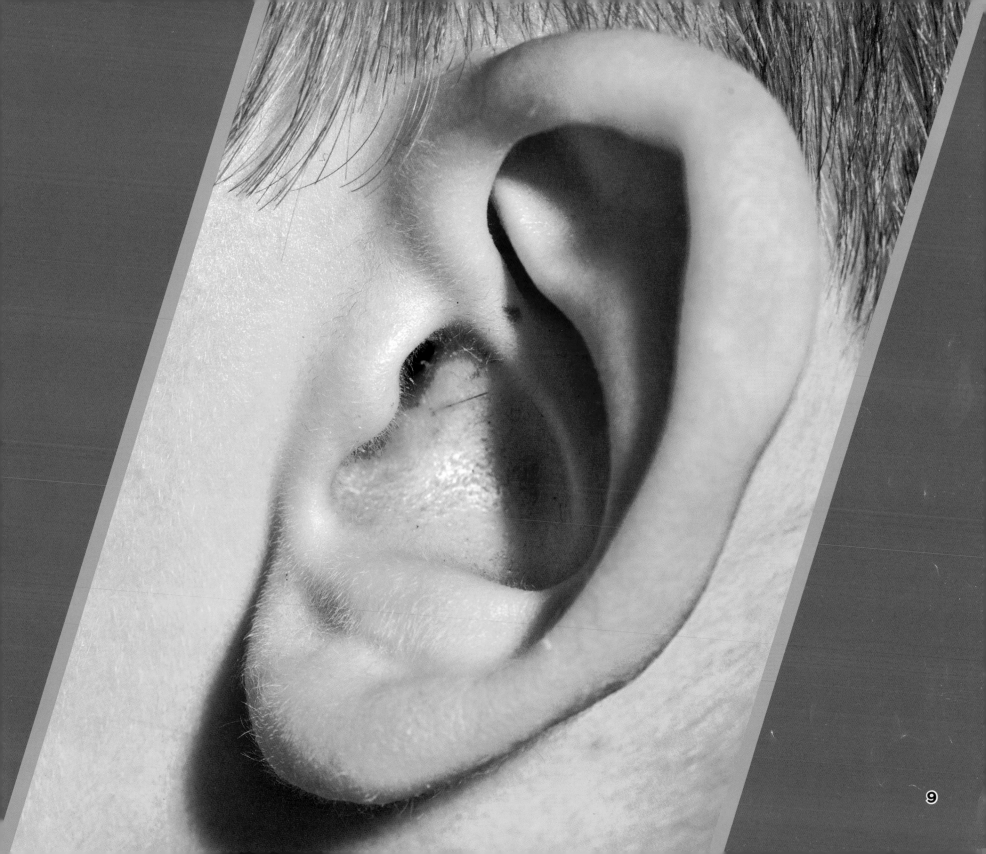

9

Mucus

Mucus, or snot, is sticky and slimy to keep dirt and germs out of your lungs. Because mucus holds germs, wash your hands after blowing your nose.

Scabs

Scabs are nature's bandages.

Don't pick at scabs.

If you do, you could let dirt

and germs into your body.

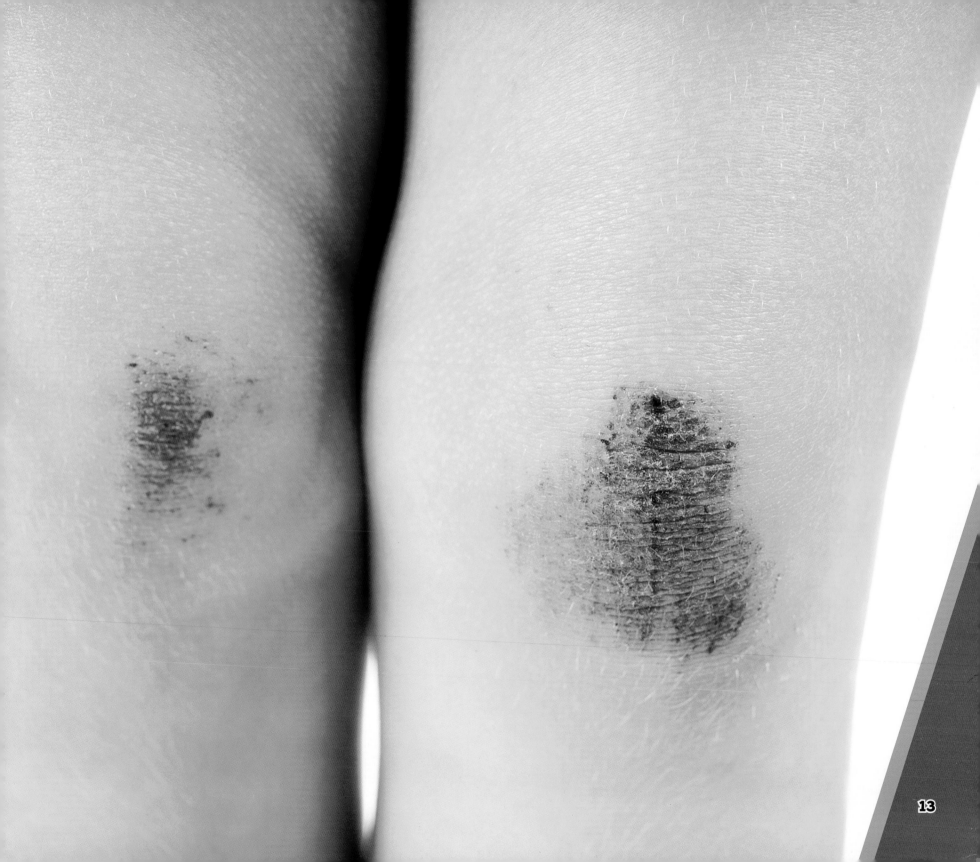

Scars

If you cut or scrape your skin,

it could grow back as a scar.

Scars are not like normal skin.

They cannot grow hair

or tan in the sun.

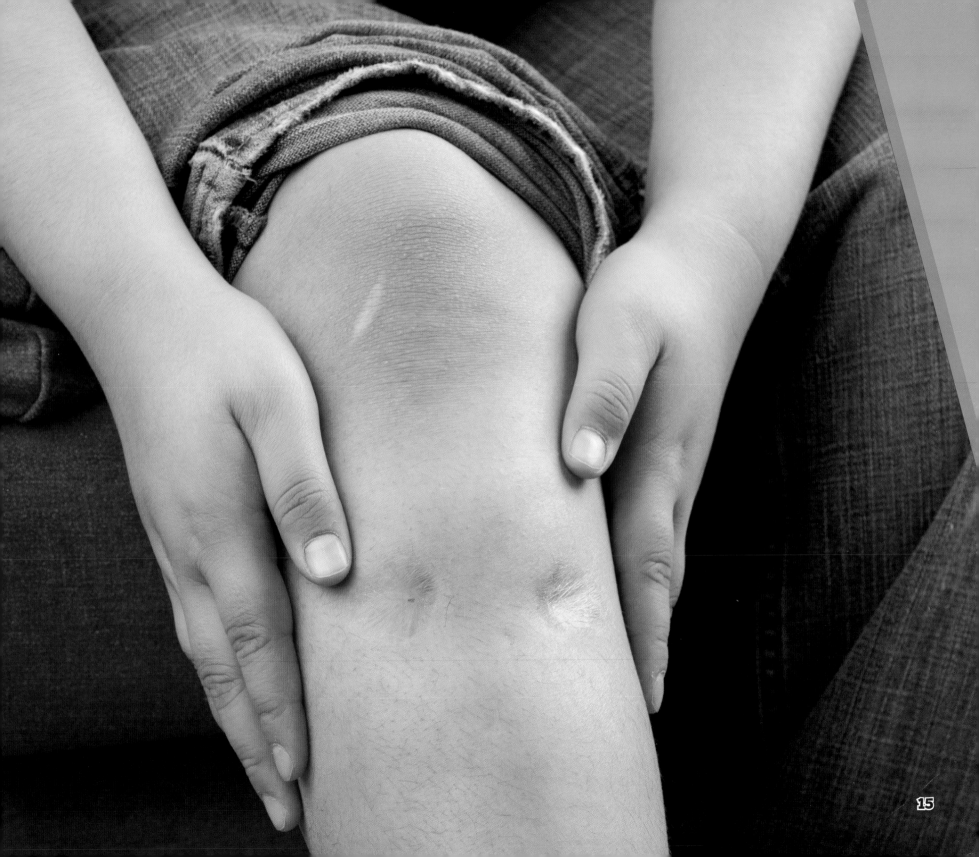

Sweat

Sweat is your body's way of cooling you down. As sweat dries, your skin feels cooler. Sweat smells because of the bacteria that grows in it.

Bad Breath

Bad breath is caused by food, tooth decay, and bacteria. A clean mouth keeps bad breath away. Brush and floss to get rid of bad breath.

Fun Facts

- If you want to have less gas, don't gobble your food. Eating fast lets a lot of air into your stomach.

- When you sneeze, air and mucus fly out of your mouth at up to 100 miles (160 kilometers) per hour.

- When you cut yourself, your blood starts to make a scab in about 10 seconds.

- When you brush your teeth, always brush your tongue too. Bacteria live there as well.

- People have millions of tiny bacteria living on them all the time. Most kinds don't make you sick or cause problems. Some kinds help you.

Glossary

bacteria—very small living things that exist all around you and inside you; some bacteria cause disease

ear canal—the passage from your outer ear to your inner ear

germ—a very small living thing that causes disease; bacteria and viruses are two common kinds of germs

sweat—a salty liquid that comes out of the small holes, or pores, in skin

tooth decay—the breaking down of teeth

Read More

Ardagh, Philip. *Your Body: Boogers and All*. New York: Price Stern Sloan, 2010.

Morgan, Sally. *How Taste Works*. Our Senses. New York: PowerKids Press, 2010.

Royston, Angela. *Ooze and Goo*. Disgusting Body Facts. Chicago: Raintree, 2010.

Internet Sites

FactHound offers a safe, fun way to find Internet sites related to this book. All of the sites on FactHound have been researched by our staff.

Here's all you do:

Visit *www.facthound.com*

Type in this code: 9781429668088

Super-cool stuff! Check out projects, games and lots more at www.capstonekids.com

Index

Word Count: 219 (main text)
Grade: 1
Early-Intervention Level: 21